Great African Americans

Langston Hughes

Great American Poet

Revised Edition

Patricia and Fredrick McKissack

Enslow Publishers, Inc.

40 Industrial Road	PO Box 38
Box 398	Aldershot
Berkeley Heights, NJ 07922	Hants GU12 6BP
USA	UK

http://www.enslow.com

To Carol Greene

Revised Edition of *Langston Hughes: Great American Poet* © 1992

Library of Congress Cataloging-in-Publication Data

McKissack, Pat, 1944–
    Langston Hughes : great American poet / Patricia and Fredrick
    McKissack. — Rev. ed.
       p. cm. — (Great African Americans)
    Includes index.
    ISBN 0-7660-1695-1
    1. Hughes, Langston, 1902–1967—Juvenile literature. 2. Poets, American—20th century—Biography—
Juvenile literature. 3. African American poets—Biography—Juvenile literature. [1. Hughes, Langston,
1902–1967. 2. Poets, American. 3. African Americans—Biography.] I. McKissack, Fredrick. II. Title.
    PS3515.U274 Z677 2002
    818'.5209—dc21

                                         00-012419

To Our Readers
We have done our best to make sure all Internet addresses in this book were active and appropriate when we went to press. However, the author and the publisher have no control over and assume no liability for the material available on those Internet sites or on other Web sites they may link to. Any comments or suggestions can be sent by e-mail to comments@enslow.com or to the address on the back cover.

Every effort has been made to locate all copyright holders of material used in this book. If any errors or omissions have occurred, corrections will be made in future editions of this book.

Selections from THE COLLECTED POEMS OF LANGSTON HUGHES by Langston Hughes, copyright © 1994 by The Estate of Langston Hughes. Used by permission of Alfred A. Knopf, a division of Random House, Inc.

Illustrations Credits: Library of Congress, pp. 11 (L), 11(R), 13, 15, 17, 25, 27; Photos from the Langston Hughes Collection at the Yale Beinecke Rare Book and Manuscript Library are published by permission of Harold Ober Asssociates, Inc., pp. 3, 6, 7, 9, 10, 14, 20, 21, 22, 26; Special Collections and Archives, W.E.B. Du Bois Library, University of Massachusetts Amherst, p. 16; United Nations, p. 19; Yale Collection of American Literature, Beinecke Rare Book and Manuscript Library, pp. 4, 24.

Cover Illustrations: Library of Congress; Photos from the Langston Hughes Collection at the Yale Beinecke Rare Book and Manuscript Library, published by permission of Harold Ober Asssociates, Inc.; Yale Collection of American Literature, Beinecke Rare Book and Manuscript Library.

TABLE OF CONTENTS

Langston Hughes
February 1, 1902–May 22, 1967

CHAPTER 1

To Mexico and Back

It was very cold in Joplin, Missouri, the day Langston Hughes was born. And his father, James Hughes, was very angry. James had studied hard to become a lawyer in Oklahoma. But a new law said that African Americans could not be lawyers there.

James wanted to do better. He thought a black man could not live a good life in the United States. So he left his wife, Carrie, and their baby, Langston, and moved to Mexico.

Carrie Hughes had been to college, too. Still, it was hard for her to find work. She and Langston had to move from place to place. At last she found a job in Kansas.

Carrie Hughes and her son, Langston, moved many times while she looked for a job.

James opened a law office down in Mexico. He had lots of work. He was doing well. He asked his family to come live with him. Langston and his mother took a train to Mexico.

Langston's father, James, worked as a lawyer in Mexico.

The day Langston and his mother arrived, there was an earthquake. The room shook. Mrs. Hughes screamed. She held little Langston closely. They had never been so frightened. Langston's mother said she would not stay another day in Mexico.

And she didn't. Langston and his mother left on the next train back to Kansas. James would not come back to the United States. The three of them never lived together again as a family.

CHAPTER 2

Listening to Stories

Langston's mother worked at all kinds of jobs. Many times she didn't make enough money to buy food or pay the rent. So when Langston was eight years old, he went to live with his grandmother, Mary Langston, in Lawrence, Kansas.

Langston missed his mother, but he loved his grandmother very much. She told wonderful stories about great African Americans like Frederick Douglass and Sojourner Truth.

The story he liked best was about Lewis Sheridan Leary. Lewis Leary was his grandmother's first husband. He was killed in 1859 at Harper's Ferry, Virginia. He had been part of John Brown's army. These men had tried to help slaves fight for their own freedom.

When Langston's grandmother told the story, she took out an old stained shawl full of holes. Lewis Leary had this shawl with him when he died. The story made Langston feel proud.

The Bible stories his grandmother told interested Langston, too. He also loved the hymns she sang.

Langston was proud to hear about the many people who worked to end slavery.

9

There were not many black children in Kansas in the early 1900s. Langston was the only black child in his class. So he made friends with people in his books. He visited far-away and wonderful places by reading his books. He also wrote poetry and stories when he felt lonely.

When he was eight, Langston went to live with his grandmother, Mary Langston.

When Langston was twelve years old, his grandmother died. For two years after that, he lived with people he lovingly called Auntie and Uncle Reed.

Then Langston's mother married Homer Clarke. Langston went to live with them. He liked his stepfather very much. It was good to be home with his mother again.

Langston finished grade

school in Lincoln, Illinois. Then Homer got a job in Cleveland, Ohio, and the family moved there. Going to school in Cleveland was much more fun for Langston. Children in his class were from different races and from other countries, too.

Grandmother Mary told stories about great African Americans like Frederick Douglass, left, and Sojourner Truth, right.

11

CHAPTER 3

Deep Like the Rivers

When Langston was in high school he heard from his father, James Hughes. He wanted Langston to spend the summer with him in Mexico. Langston was surprised. He had not heard from his father in years. Langston went to Mexico on the train.

James had done very well. He owned a big ranch and had lots of workers. But James was a bitter, angry man. He said unkind things to people.

12

Cleveland in 1916 was a fast-growing city. Langston liked his school there. He met many different kinds of people.

Langston ran on his high school track team.

When summer was over, Langston was happy to go home.

In 1920, Langston graduated from Cleveland Central High School. His father wanted him to come back to Mexico. Langston went because he wanted to go to college. He did not have money to pay for it and he needed help.

On his way to Mexico he crossed the Mississippi River. The dark water made him think about his race. So he wrote a poem called "The Negro Speaks of Rivers." It began: *My soul has grown deep like the rivers.*

The poem was printed in *The Crisis* magazine in 1921. For the first time, many people got to read his poetry.

James Hughes decided to pay for Langston's college. He sent him to study mining engineering at Columbia University in New York City.

Near Columbia University is a mostly black neighborhood called Harlem. Living close to Harlem made Langston feel like part of a large black family. He enjoyed being around other African Americans.

In 1921, Langston took classes at Columbia University. This is the school library.

15

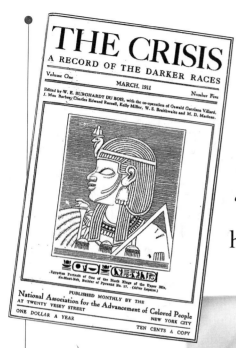

He liked the sounds and smells, the music and dance, the way people talked to each other. He decided to live in Harlem and write about it. He wrote the poem "My People" to show how much he loved being black:

Many people read Langston's poetry in The Crisis.

The night is beautiful,
So the faces of my people.

The stars are beautiful,
So the eyes of my people.

Beautiful, also, is the sun.
Beautiful, also, are the souls of my people.

Langston loved the excitement of the streets of Harlem.

CHAPTER 4

The Weary Blues

L angston loved New York City, but he didn't like school. He soon quit. Langston never heard from his father again. When James Hughes died, he didn't leave his son anything. Langston felt sorry for his father, because he had been such a sad and lonely man.

When Langston was twenty-one years old, he joined the crew of the S.S. *West Hesseltine*. The ship sailed from New York to West Africa.

Langston was happy to visit Africa. At this street market, women are selling many kinds of fruits and vegetables.

Young Langston was excited about seeing the places he had read about in books.

Africa was exciting. So were many of the people he met. The bright clothes, music, and dancing of Africa made him think of Harlem. He wrote "Color," a poem that says African Americans should be proud of their skin color:

When he was twenty-four, Langston decided to go back to college.

Wear it
Like a banner
For the proud
Not like a shroud.
Wear it
Like a song
Soaring high
Not moan or cry.

20

After he left Africa, Langston went to Holland, and then to Paris. He worked hard washing dishes and scrubbing floors to earn money. But he always found time to write.

Finally Langston's travels brought him back to New York City. The first place he went to was Harlem. He laughed for joy! He felt at home. But Langston's mother was living in

Hughes, left, liked to travel. His adventures took him to many exciting places.

Washington, D.C., at that time. He wanted to be near her, so he moved to Washington in 1925.

Langston was working as a busboy at a hotel—but he wrote poems in his free time.

Langston worked as a busboy at a hotel in Washington. Once, a very famous poet named Vachel Lindsay was staying at the hotel. So Langston put some of his poems next to the poet's dinner plate.

Later that night, many people came to hear Vachel Lindsay read his poems. He read Langston's poems, too. He said he had discovered a new poet.

Newspapers across the country wrote about Lindsay's poetry reading. Soon many people knew about the new black poet, Langston Hughes.

CHAPTER 5

Harlem's Poet

In 1926 Langston won a prize for his first book of poems, *The Weary Blues*. His poems were about Harlem life.

The Great Depression began in 1929. Times were very hard. Black people left the South and came north looking for work. But there were no jobs.

During the 1930s, Harlem was becoming overcrowded. People were hungry and angry. Many were homeless. Langston wrote about the

During his life, Langston wrote ten books of poetry, sixty short stories, two books about his life, children's books, and many plays.

people he saw on Harlem streets, in churches, in schools, in clubs. He wrote about their pain and joy. He wrote about their anger and love.

Langston kept writing during the 1940s and 1950s. He always enjoyed the music of Harlem. He invited musicians to play jazz, spirituals, and blues music while he read his work in public. His poetry was like music.

During the 1950s, Langston wrote stories about

Jesse B. Semple, who was called "Simple." Even though he was not a real person, he seemed real.

Simple had a way of saying funny things that sometimes had a serious meaning. People liked reading about this down-to-earth man who worked hard and lived in Harlem. Simple knew how to enjoy life, even if he didn't have a lot of money.

Langston loved art and music, too. Here he holds a Mexican sculpture.

Langston had written more than five Simple books by 1957. Langston also wrote two books about his own life: *The Big Sea* and *I Wonder As I Wander*. And he won many awards.

Langston traveled to many of the places he read about as a child. But most of all, he liked coming

25

The famous poet was loved by people of all ages.

home to 127th Street in Harlem. He did such a good job of writing about the people who lived in this neighborhood that he was sometimes called "Harlem's Poet." But Langston Hughes belonged to all Americans.

He wrote until he died on May 22, 1967. A jazz band played at his funeral. He had told his friends not to be sad. He wanted them to keep working for the better world he dreamed about. Today, Langston Hughes's poetry still sings to us about dreams:

Hold fast to dreams
For if dreams die
Life is a broken-winged bird
That cannot fly.

Hold fast to dreams
For when dreams go
Life is a barren field
Frozen with snow.

timeLine

1902 ~ Born on February 1 in Joplin, Missouri.

1920 ~ Graduates from Central High School in Cleveland, Ohio.

1921 ~ First published poem; begins college at Columbia University.

1921

1926 ~ First book, *The Weary Blues*, published; enters Lincoln University.

1927 ~ Graduates from Lincoln University.

1930 ~ First novel, *Not Without Laughter*, published.

1932 ~ Children's books, *The Dream Keeper* and *Popo and Fifina*, published.

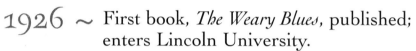

1925

1940 ~ Publishes a book about his life, *The Big Sea*.

1956 ~ Second book about his life, *I Wonder As I Wander*, is published.

1960 ~ Receives the Spingarn Medal from the National Association for the Advancement of Colored People (NAACP).

1967 ~ Dies in New York City on May 22.

WORDS to KNOW

blues—Music about life's troubles and sorrows.

earthquake—A trembling or shaking of the ground. Earthquakes are caused by a clashing of the plates of rock deep in the earth, making the ground shift and move. Earthquakes destroy buildings and homes. People can be hurt or killed, too.

graduate—To complete a course of study at a school.

Great Depression—A period of about ten years, starting in 1929, when many banks, factories, and stores went out of business. Millions of people lost their jobs and sometimes their homes, too. They were poor and unhappy because it was so hard for them to pay for food and other things they needed.

Harlem—A mostly black neighborhood in New York City. During the 1920s and 1930s, many black poets, writers, and artists lived and worked there. This time was called the Harlem Renaissance.

jazz—Music with a strong rhythm, used to show feelings and ideas. Jazz is mainly performed with instruments, and the musicians often make up new parts as they play the music.

29

WORDS TO KNOW

mining engineering—Mining engineers figure out the best way to get ore and oil out of the ground and out of rock so it can be used by people. Gold is an example of an ore.

National Association for the Advancement of Colored People (NAACP)—An organization started to help all Americans gain equal rights and protection under the law.

poetry—A form of writing that uses any combination of colorful words, rhythm, and rhyme, written in verse. Poetry uses images or word pictures to express emotions and ideas.

slaves—People who are owned by other people and are forced to work without pay. In America, slavery lasted from 1619 to 1865.

spirituals—Religious songs that were sung by black slaves. Now they are enjoyed and sung by people all over the world.

LEARN MORE about LANGSTON HUGHES

Books

Cooper, Floyd. *Coming Home: From the Life of Langston Hughes*. New York: Penguin Putnam Books for Young Readers, 1998.

Hughes, Langston. *The Dream Keeper and Other Poems*. New York: Random House, Inc., 1997.

Walker, Alice. *Langston Hughes, American Poet*. New York: HarperCollins Children's Book Group, 1998.

Internet Addresses

The Academy of American Poets
Biography, poems.

<http://www.poets.org/poets/poets.cfm?prmID=84>

Red Hot Jazz
Biography and photos.

<http://www.redhotjazz.com/hughes.html>

index